FRIED TO PERFECTION

THE ULTIMATE GUIDE TO AIR FRYER COOKING

JOHN R. SCOTT

Copyright © 2024 JOHN R. SCOTT

All rights reserved. No part of this publication may be reproduced, distributed, or transmitted in any form or by any means, including photocopying, recording, or other electronic or mechanical methods, without the prior written permission of the publisher, except in the case of brief quotations embodied in critical reviews and certain other noncommercial uses permitted by copyright law.

Table of Contents

INTRODUCTION 4
   BRIEF HISTORY AND EXPLANATION OF HOW AIR FRYERS WORK 6
   BENEFITS OF USING AN AIR FRYER FOR HEALTHIER COOKING 9
   Overview of what readers can expect from the cookbook 12
   EXPLANATION OF DIFFERENT TYPES OF AIR FRYERS AND HOW TO CHOOSE THE RIGHT ONE 15

ESSENTIAL TIPS AND TRICKS FOR SUCCESSFUL AIR FRYING 19
   COMMON MISTAKES TO AVOID WHEN USING AN AIR FRYER 22
   SAFETY PRECAUTIONS AND MAINTENANCE OF AIR FRYERS 25

BREAKFAST 29
   RECIPES FOR DELICIOUS AND HEALTHY BREAKFAST OPTIONS 29

LUNCH 44

QUICK AND EASY LUNCH RECIPES SUITABLE FOR BUSY SCHEDULES 44

DINNER 55

FLAVORFUL DINNER RECIPES FOR THE WHOLE FAMILY 55

SNACKS 64

SNACK RECIPES PERFECT FOR ANY TIME OF THE DAY 64

DESSERTS / SMOOTHIES 82

INDULGENT DESSERTS AND REFRESHING SMOOTHIE RECIPES MADE HEALTHIER WITH THE AIR FRYER 82

MEAL PLAN 91

CONCLUSION 94

Final thoughts on deep fryer cooking and its versatility 94

Encouragement for readers to explore and experiment with their fryers 95

Thanking Readers for Joining the Air Fryer Cookbook Cooking Journey 96

INTRODUCTION

Welcome to Fried to Perfection: The Ultimate Guide to Air Fryer Cooking, a culinary adventure that promises to redefine the way you approach home cooking. In the hustle and bustle of our modern lives, the desire for delicious and healthy foods often collides with time constraints and healthy choices. But don't worry because the air fryer is here to revolutionize your kitchen.

In this comprehensive guide, we delve into the world of air frying - an innovative cooking technique that offers the exciting flavors and textures of traditional frying with a fraction of the oil and calories. With the deep fryer as your culinary ally, you'll discover a new realm of possibilities, from crispy starters to juicy main courses and delicious desserts - all prepared with ease and precision.

But before we dive into the recipes and techniques that will up your cooking game, take a moment to demystify the art of air frying. At its core, air frying uses the power of circulating hot air to cook food evenly, creating that coveted crispy surface without the need for excess oil. It's a game-changer for health-conscious cooks and busy families alike, offering a guilt-free way to enjoy your favorite fried foods.

In this guide you will find everything you need to become a deep fryer lover. Each page is designed to inspire and delight your taste buds, from basic tips and tricks for mastering your air fryer to a diverse range of recipes covering breakfast, lunch, dinner, snacks and desserts. Whether you're new to the kitchen or a seasoned cook, there's something for everyone here.

So join me on this culinary journey as we uncover the full potential of deep fryer cooking. Together, we'll discover that perfection isn't just a lofty goal—it's something that can be achieved, fried to perfection, one delicious dish at a time.

BRIEF HISTORY AND EXPLANATION OF HOW AIR FRYERS WORK

In the ever-evolving landscape of kitchen appliances, few innovations have captured the imagination as much as the air fryer. As we embark on our "Fried to Perfection: The Ultimate Guide to Air Fryer Cooking" culinary journey, it's only fitting that we begin with a brief exploration of the history and mechanics of this revolutionary device.

The concept of air frying can be traced back to the late 20th century when the desire for healthier cooking alternatives began to gain momentum. In response to growing concerns about the health risks associated with traditional frying methods, innovators set out to devise a solution that would deliver the same crispy and indulgent results without the need for excessive amounts of oil.

Enter the deep fryer - a compact tabletop appliance that uses the power of circulating hot air to cook food to crispy perfection. At the heart of the fryer is a powerful heating element and a high-speed fan, which work together to quickly circulate hot air around the food. This circulating air creates a convection effect, crisping the outer layer of food while retaining moisture and flavor.

Arguably the magic of the air fryer, however, is its ability to achieve that coveted golden-brown crispiness with only a fraction of the oil usually required for deep-frying. By using minimal oil and relying instead on the natural fats present in the food itself, the air fryer offers a healthier alternative to traditional frying methods without sacrificing flavor or texture.

As we delve deeper into the mechanics of air frying over the following pages, we'll explore the myriad benefits and possibilities this innovative cooking technique offers. From crispy chicken wings to perfectly roasted vegetables, the air fryer opens up a world of culinary possibilities, allowing home cooks to enjoy their favorite deep-fried treats guilt-free.

So, dear reader, as we embark on this journey through the world of deep fryer cooking, let us marvel at the ingenuity and innovation that has brought us to this moment. From its humble beginnings to its status as a kitchen essential, the deep fryer represents the perfect combination of health, convenience and culinary pleasure. Welcome to 'Fried to Perfection' where we explore the art and science of deep fryer cooking in all its crispy golden glory.

BENEFITS OF USING AN AIR FRYER FOR HEALTHIER COOKING

We're on a mission to uncover the secrets to healthier cooking without sacrificing taste or satisfaction. In this introduction, we'll dive into the many benefits of using an air fryer and explore how this innovative kitchen appliance can help you achieve your health and wellness goals without compromising on taste.

1. **Reduced oil consumption:** One of the most significant benefits of deep frying is its ability to drastically reduce the amount of oil needed to achieve crispy, golden brown results. Traditional frying methods often rely on submerging food in large amounts of oil, resulting in a high calorie and fat content. In contrast, air frying requires only a fraction of the oil, making it a much healthier alternative for those looking to reduce added fat in their diet.

2. Healthier cooking methods: By using hot air circulation to cook food, air fryers eliminate the need for deep frying, which can lead to the formation of harmful compounds such as acrylamide. Plus, air frying requires minimal added fat, making it an ideal choice for those looking to reduce their saturated fat and cholesterol intake. With a hot air fryer, you can enjoy all the flavor and texture of your favorite fried foods without the associated health risks.

3. Preserved Nutrients: Unlike traditional frying methods, which can result in nutrient loss due to high heat and long cooking times, air frying preserves the nutritional integrity of your ingredients. By cooking food quickly and evenly, air fryers help retain essential vitamins and minerals, ensuring your meals are as nutritious as they are tasty.

4. Versatility: In addition to the health benefits, deep-fryer cooking offers unparalleled versatility, allowing you to easily prepare a wide variety of dishes. From crunchy appetizers to juicy main courses and even delicious desserts, the possibilities are endless with a deep fryer at your disposal. Whether you crave classic comfort foods or experiment with new flavors and ingredients, the deep fryer will surely become your kitchen companion.

In 'Fried to Perfection' we explore these benefits in more detail and provide you with expert tips, delicious recipes and step-by-step instructions on how to get the most out of your fryer. So if you're ready to embark on a journey to healthier and tastier cooking, join us as we explore the endless possibilities of the deep fryer kitchen.

OVERVIEW OF WHAT READERS CAN EXPECT FROM THE COOKBOOK

In the busy landscape of the modern kitchen, where time is a precious commodity and health-conscious choices rule, "Fried to Perfection: The Ultimate Guide to Air Fryer Cooking" emerges as a beacon of culinary innovation. In the pages of this cookbook, readers will embark on an exciting journey into the world of air frying – a culinary revolution that promises to change the way we cook and enjoy our favorite foods.

But what exactly can readers expect from this comprehensive guide to deep fryer cooking? Let me provide an interesting overview:

Culinary Exploration: Get ready for a culinary adventure like no other as we delve into the art and science of air frying. From the basics of air fryer operation to advanced techniques to up your cooking game, this cookbook leaves no stone unturned in its quest to unlock the full potential of the air fryer kitchen.

Delicious Recipes: Get ready to tantalize your taste buds with a collection of recipes carefully crafted to showcase the versatility and flavor of air frying. From hearty breakfasts to satisfying dinners, indulgent snacks to decadent desserts, each recipe is a celebration of culinary creativity and innovation.

Mastering Ingredients: Discover the power of simple, healthy ingredients as we explore the building blocks of deep fryer cooking. Learn how to get the most out of every ingredient and easily create memorable meals, from fresh produce to succulent meats, pantry staples to exotic spices.

Step-by-step instructions: Whether you're a seasoned cook or new to the kitchen, don't worry—this cookbook is designed to guide you every step of the way. With clear, concise instructions and helpful tips, you'll feel confident and able to tackle any recipe with ease.

Cooking Time and Temperature Instructions: Say goodbye to guesswork and welcome precision with our comprehensive cooking time and temperature instructions. No more undercooked food or burnt edges - just perfectly cooked food every time.

Adapting standard recipes: Love your favorite recipes but want to make them healthier and more convenient? With our expert tips on adapting standard air fryer recipes, you'll learn how to transform old favorites into new classics, all while saving time and calories.

Inspiration and Creativity: Get ready to unleash your inner culinary artist as we inspire you to get creative with deep fryer cooking. From flavor-packed marinades to innovative ingredient combinations, the possibilities are endless—and the results are sure to impress.

In Fried to Perfection, readers will not only discover the joy and convenience of deep-fryer cooking, but also embark on a journey of culinary discovery and self-discovery. So, whether you're a seasoned cook looking to expand your repertoire or a kitchen newbie eager to learn new skills, prepare to be inspired, delighted and completely captivated by the delicious world of deep fryer cooking.

EXPLANATION OF DIFFERENT TYPES OF AIR FRYERS AND HOW TO CHOOSE THE RIGHT ONE

When it comes to deep fryer cooking, choosing the right equipment can be critical to culinary success. With a variety of options available on the market, each boasting their own unique features and capabilities, it's essential to understand the different types of air fryer and how to choose the perfect one for your needs. Let's dive into this exploration on the pages of "Fried to Perfection: The Ultimate Guide to Air Fryer Cooking."

Basket Style Fryers: This is the most common type of fryer with a basket or drawer where the food is placed for cooking. They usually come in a variety of sizes, from compact models suitable for single servings to larger units ideal for family meals. Basket-style fryers offer the versatility to cook a wide variety of foods, from fries and chicken wings to vegetables and even baked goods.

Oven-Style Air Fryers: Also known as air fryers or convection ovens, these appliances resemble traditional toaster ovens but with the added function of air frying. They offer more cooking space compared to basket fryers, making them suitable for larger quantities or larger pieces of food such as whole chickens or pizzas. Air fryer ovens often come with additional features such as a grill function or multiple cooking grates, increasing their versatility in the kitchen.

Hybrid Air Fryers: Combining the functions of traditional air frying with other cooking methods such as pressure cooking or slow cooking, hybrid air fryers offer the ultimate in convenience and versatility. These multifunctional appliances allow you to experiment with different cooking techniques and create a wide variety of dishes without cluttering up your kitchen with multiple appliances.

Toaster Oven Air Fryers: These devices are a hybrid between a toaster oven and a hot air fryer, offering the convenience of toasting bread or baking while also providing air frying options. They are suitable for small kitchens or for individuals who want to make their kitchen appliances more efficient without sacrificing functionality.

Accessories and attachments: Some air fryers come with additional accessories or attachments, such as grill grates, baking trays or skewers, which further expand their versatility. When choosing a deep fryer, consider whether these extra features match your cooking preferences and the types of food you plan to prepare.

There are several factors to consider when choosing the right deep fryer for your kitchen:

Capacity: Determine the size of your air fryer based on the size of your household and the amount of food you usually cook. A larger capacity may be more suitable for families or those who entertain frequently, while smaller units are ideal for singles or couples.

Features: Consider the features offered by different fryer models, such as temperature control, pre-programmed cooking settings, digital displays and easy cleaning. Choose a model that offers the features you need for your cooking style and preferences.

Budget: Set a budget for buying a deep fryer and compare prices on different brands and models. While more expensive models may offer additional features or higher capacities, there are also affordable options available that provide excellent performance.

Reviews and Recommendations: Explore online reviews and find recommendations from friends or family members who own deep fryers. Reading first-hand experiences can help you make an informed decision and ensure that the fryer you choose meets your expectations.

By understanding the different types of air fryers and considering these factors, you can confidently choose the perfect device to embark on your deep frying journey. Whether you opt for a cupcake style fryer, an oven model or a hybrid appliance, rest assured that 'Fried to

Perfection' will guide you through the culinary possibilities that await and ensure that every meal you create will be a masterpiece, taste and texture.

ESSENTIAL TIPS AND TRICKS FOR SUCCESSFUL AIR FRYING

Preheat your air fryer: As with traditional ovens, preheating your air fryer ensures that your food cooks evenly and crisps perfectly. Preheat for about 3-5 minutes before adding ingredients.

Use the right oil: While one of the benefits of air frying is using less oil, choosing the right oil can improve flavor and texture. Choose oils with a high smoke point, such as avocado oil, peanut oil, or grape seed oil.

Do not overcrowd the basket: For crispy results, ensure there is enough space between the foods in the air fryer basket. Overfilling can lead to uneven cooking and soggy results.

Shake or flip the food in the middle: For even cooking, shake the basket or turn the food halfway through the cooking process. This helps ensure that all sides are evenly browned.

Experiment with spices and marinades: Air-frying is a fantastic way to add flavour to food. Experiment with different flavourings, herbs and spices, or marinate the ingredients ahead of time for extra flavour.

Use parchment paper or aluminium foil: To prevent food from sticking to the basket and make cleaning easier, consider lining your air fryer basket with parchment paper or aluminium foil. Be sure to poke several holes in the paper or foil to ensure proper air circulation.

Monitor cooking time: Air fryers cook food faster than traditional methods, so keep a close eye on your food to avoid overcooking. It's a good idea to check the food a few minutes before the suggested cooking time and adjust as needed.

Use accessories: Many air fryers come with accessories such as racks, skewers, and baking trays. Experiment with this accessory to expand your air-frying repertoire and prepare a variety of dishes with ease.

Clean the fryer regularly: To maintain optimal performance and prevent unwanted flavours from transferring between dishes, clean the fryer after each use. Most parts are dishwasher safe or can easily be hand washed with warm soapy water.

Get creative: Don't be afraid to think outside the box and get creative with your fryer. From crunchy snacks to delicious desserts, the possibilities of cooking in a deep fryer are endless.

By following these basic tips and tricks, you'll be well on your way to mastering the art of air frying and creating delicious, crispy dishes with ease.

COMMON MISTAKES TO AVOID WHEN USING AN AIR FRYER

In the pursuit of culinary perfection in your air fryer, there are a few common pitfalls that even the most experienced cooks can run into. Here are some mistakes to avoid to ensure your air-frying efforts are indeed fried to perfection:

Overfilling the basket: It can be tempting to pack as much food as possible into the fryer basket, but overcrowding can impede air circulation, leading to uneven cooking and soggy results. To ensure crispiness, arrange the ingredients in a single layer, leaving some space between each piece.

Forgetting to preheat: As with traditional ovens, preheating your fryer is essential for optimal cooking results. Skipping this step can result in longer cooking times and less evenly cooked food. For best results, take a few extra minutes to preheat the fryer.

Ingredients don't dry out: Excess moisture on your ingredients can prevent them from achieving the desired crunchy texture. Be sure to dry the ingredients with paper towels to remove excess moisture before air-frying.

Using too much oil: While air frying requires less oil than traditional frying methods, it's still possible to overdo it. Using too much oil can result in greasy and soggy food. For best results, keep the coats light or use an oil spray.

Neglecting to shake or flip: To ensure even cooking and crispness on all sides, it is important to shake or flip the ingredients halfway through the cooking process. This helps redistribute the heat and ensures that every bite is perfectly fried.

Cooking over-breaded foods: While air fryers can produce beautifully crispy results, they can struggle with foods that are heavily breaded or breaded. For better results, choose a lighter coating or consider using alternative coatings such as panko breadcrumbs.

Essential maintenance and cleaning: Like any kitchen appliance, your deep fryer requires regular maintenance to keep it working at its best. Failure to clean the fryer after each use or to remove accumulated grease and food particles can affect its performance and lifespan.

By avoiding these common mistakes and following the tips and techniques outlined in "Fried to Perfection: The Ultimate Guide to Air Fryer Cooking," you'll be well on your way to air fryer success. With a little patience, practice and a healthy dose of experimentation, you'll soon fall in love with crispy, delicious meals that are truly fried to perfection.

SAFETY PRECAUTIONS AND MAINTENANCE OF AIR FRYERS

When embarking on the air fryer journey with "Fried to Perfection: The Ultimate Guide to Air Fryer Cooking," it's essential to prioritize safety and proper maintenance to ensure not only delicious dishes, but also the longevity of your trusty kitchen companion. Here are some basic safety precautions and maintenance tips to keep in mind:

SECURITY PRECAUTIONS:

Read the instructions: Before using the deep fryer for the first time, read the manufacturer's instructions and the safety manual thoroughly. Familiarize yourself with the specific features and functions of your deep fryer to ensure safe and correct use.

Placing on a stable surface: Always place the fryer on a stable, heat-resistant surface away from edges or overhanging cabinets. Make sure there is enough space around the fryer for proper air circulation and ventilation.

Avoid Overfilling: To prevent overheating and uneven cooking, avoid overfilling the air fryer basket with ingredients. For optimal results, follow the recommended maximum capacity guidelines provided by the manufacturer.

Be careful with hot surfaces: Be careful when handling hot surfaces, including the basket and tray, during and after cooking. Use oven mitts or heat resistant gloves to protect your hands and prevent burns.

Keep away from water: Never immerse the fryer in water or other liquids, as this could damage the device and pose a safety hazard. Clean the removable parts separately according to the manufacturer's instructions.

Monitor during operation: Always supervise the fryer during operation, especially when cooking at high temperatures. Do not place flammable materials or utensils near the fryer and never leave it unattended while it is in use.

Use the correct accessories: Use only accessories and attachments specifically designed for use with your deep fryer. Use of incompatible accessories may compromise performance and safety.

MAINTENANCE TIPS:

Regular cleaning: After each use, allow the fryer to cool completely before cleaning. Remove the basket and tray and wash them in warm soapy water or put them in the dishwasher if they are dishwasher safe. Wipe the inside and outside of the fryer with a damp cloth to remove food residue or grease.

Deep Cleaning: Regularly deep clean your fryer to remove stubborn stains or residue. Refer to the manufacturer's instructions for specific cleaning recommendations, such as using vinegar or baking soda solutions for stubborn stains.

Inspect for damage: Regularly inspect the power cord, plug, and other fryer components for signs of damage or wear. If you notice any problems, stop using immediately and contact the manufacturer for repair or replacement parts.

Proper storage: When the fryer is not in use, store it in a cool, dry place away from direct sunlight and moisture. Do not store it near heat sources or in confined spaces where air circulation may be restricted.

By following these safety precautions and maintenance tips, you can enjoy the convenience and versatility of air frying with peace of mind, knowing you're cooking safely and preserving the life of your beloved air fryer.

BREAKFAST

RECIPES FOR DELICIOUS AND HEALTHY BREAKFAST OPTIONS

✦ Air-Fried Breakfast Burritos

Ingredients: Tortillas, eggs, bell peppers, onions, cheese, cooked sausage or bacon, salsa (optional)

Instructions: Scramble eggs with chopped vegetables and cooked sausage or bacon. Spoon mixture onto tortillas, sprinkle with cheese, and roll into burritos. Air fry at 350°F for 5-7 minutes, until golden and crispy.

Cooking Time: 5-7 minutes

Other: Serve with salsa for dipping.

✦ Crispy Hash Browns

Ingredients: Potatoes, olive oil, salt, pepper, paprika (optional)

Instructions: Grate potatoes and toss with olive oil, salt, pepper, and paprika. Spread in a single layer in the air fryer basket. Air fry at 380°F for 15-20 minutes, flipping halfway through, until golden and crispy.

Cooking Time: 15-20 minutes

Other: Serve as a side dish or base for breakfast bowls.

✤ Cinnamon French Toast Sticks

Ingredients: Bread slices, eggs, milk, cinnamon, vanilla extract, maple syrup (optional)

Instructions: Cut bread slices into strips. Whisk together eggs, milk, cinnamon, and vanilla extract. Dip bread strips into the egg mixture and place in the air fryer basket. Air fry at 350°F for 6-8 minutes, until golden and crispy.

Cooking Time: 6-8 minutes

Other: Serve with maple syrup for dipping.

⁕ Blueberry Pancake Bites

Ingredients: Pancake batter, fresh blueberries

Instructions: Fill mini muffin cups halfway with pancake batter. Add a few blueberries to each cup. Air fry at 350°F for 5-7 minutes, until golden and cooked through.

Cooking Time: 5-7 minutes

Other: Serve as a grab-and-go breakfast option.

⁕ Spinach and Feta Egg Muffins

Ingredients: Eggs, spinach, feta cheese, cherry tomatoes, salt, pepper

Instructions: Whisk together eggs and season with salt and pepper. Stir in chopped spinach, crumbled feta cheese, and halved cherry tomatoes. Pour mixture into greased muffin cups. Air fry at 350°F for 10-12 minutes, until set.

Cooking Time: 10-12 minutes

Other: Perfect for meal prep and on-the-go breakfasts.

✤ Banana Nut Oatmeal Cups

Ingredients: Rolled oats, ripe bananas, milk, maple syrup, chopped nuts

Instructions: Mash bananas and mix with rolled oats, milk, maple syrup, and chopped nuts. Spoon mixture into greased muffin cups. Air fry at 350°F for 12-15 minutes, until golden and firm.

Cooking Time: 12-15 minutes

Other: Serve warm or chilled for a nutritious breakfast option.

✤ Apple Cinnamon Breakfast Bars

Ingredients: Rolled oats, applesauce, diced apples, cinnamon, honey, chopped nuts

Instructions: Mix rolled oats, applesauce, diced apples, cinnamon, honey, and chopped nuts until well combined. Press mixture into a greased baking dish. Air fry at 350°F for 15-20 minutes, until golden and set.

Cooking Time: 15-20 minutes

Other: Slice into bars for a convenient breakfast option.

✢ Greek Yogurt Parfait

Ingredients: Greek yogurt, granola, fresh berries, honey

Instructions: Layer Greek yogurt, granola, and fresh berries in serving glasses or jars. Drizzle with honey. Serve immediately or refrigerate for later.

Cooking Time: No cooking required

Other: Customize with your favorite fruits and toppings.

✢ Vegetable Frittata

Ingredients: Eggs, bell peppers, onions, spinach, cherry tomatoes, feta cheese, salt, pepper

Instructions: Whisk together eggs and season with salt and pepper. Stir in chopped vegetables and crumbled feta cheese. Pour mixture into greased baking dish. Air fry at 350°F for 12-15 minutes, until set.

Cooking Time: 12-15 minutes

Other: Slice into wedges and serve warm or chilled.

♣ Peanut Butter Banana Toast

Ingredients: Bread slices, peanut butter, ripe bananas, honey (optional)

Instructions: Spread peanut butter onto bread slices. Top with sliced bananas and drizzle with honey, if desired. Place in the air fryer basket. Air fry at 350°F for 3-5 minutes, until bread is toasted and toppings are warm.

Cooking Time: 3-5 minutes

Other: Enjoy as a quick and satisfying breakfast or snack.

⁂ Sausage and Egg Breakfast Sandwich

Ingredients: English muffins, cooked sausage patties, eggs, cheese slices

Instructions: Cook sausage patties and fried eggs in the air fryer. Assemble sandwiches with English muffins, sausage, eggs, and cheese slices. Wrap in foil and air fry at 350°F for 3-5 minutes, until heated through.

Cooking Time: 3-5 minutes

Other: Perfect for a hearty breakfast on the go.

⁂ Breakfast Quesadillas

Ingredients: Flour tortillas, scrambled eggs, cooked bacon or sausage, shredded cheese, salsa

Instructions: Layer scrambled eggs, cooked bacon or sausage, and shredded cheese on half of each tortilla. Fold tortillas in half to form quesadillas. Air fry at 350°F for 4-6 minutes, until cheese is melted and tortillas are crispy.

Cooking Time: 4-6 minutes

Other: Serve with salsa and sour cream for dipping.

⁕ Sweet Potato Hash

Ingredients: Sweet potatoes, bell peppers, onions, olive oil, salt, pepper, paprika

Instructions: Dice sweet potatoes, bell peppers, and onions. Toss with olive oil, salt, pepper, and paprika. Spread in a single layer in the air fryer basket. Air fry at 380°F for 15-20 minutes, tossing halfway through, until golden and crispy.

Cooking Time: 15-20 minutes

Other: Serve as a flavorful and nutritious breakfast side dish.

⁕ Avocado Toast with Poached Eggs

Ingredients: Bread slices, ripe avocados, eggs, salt, pepper, red pepper flakes (optional)

Instructions: Toast bread slices until golden. Mash ripe avocados and spread onto toast. Prepare poached eggs and place on top of avocado toast. Season with salt, pepper, and red pepper flakes, if desired.

Cooking Time: Varies based on poaching method

Other: Garnish with fresh herbs or microgreens for extra flavor.

✛ Egg and Veggie Breakfast Tacos

Ingredients: Corn tortillas, scrambled eggs, sautéed vegetables (bell peppers, onions, mushrooms), salsa, avocado slices

Instructions: Fill corn tortillas with scrambled eggs and sautéed vegetables. Top with salsa and avocado slices. Warm in the air fryer at 350°F for 3-5 minutes, until heated through.

Cooking Time: 3-5 minutes

Other: Customize with your favorite taco toppings.

♦ Breakfast Pizza

Ingredients: Pizza dough, scrambled eggs, cooked bacon or sausage, shredded cheese, sliced tomatoes, fresh herbs

Instructions: Roll out pizza dough and top with scrambled eggs, cooked bacon or sausage, shredded cheese, sliced tomatoes, and fresh herbs. Air fry at 350°F for 10-12 minutes, until crust is golden and cheese is melted.

Cooking Time: 10-12 minutes

Other: Slice and serve for a unique breakfast twist.

♦ Coconut Chia Seed Pudding

Ingredients: Coconut milk, chia seeds, honey, fresh berries, shredded coconut

Instructions: Mix coconut milk, chia seeds, and honey until well combined. Refrigerate for at least 4 hours or overnight, until thickened. Serve topped with fresh berries and shredded coconut.

Cooking Time: No cooking required

Other: A make-ahead option for busy mornings.

⁕ Breakfast Stuffed Peppers

Ingredients: Bell peppers, scrambled eggs, cooked quinoa, cooked sausage or bacon, shredded cheese

Instructions: Cut bell peppers in half and remove seeds. Fill each pepper half with scrambled eggs, cooked quinoa, cooked sausage or bacon, and shredded cheese. Air fry at 350°F for 8-10 minutes, until peppers are tender and filling is heated through.

Cooking Time: 8-10 minutes

Other: Serve as a colorful and nutritious breakfast option.

⁕ Pumpkin Spice Waffles

Ingredients: Waffle batter, pumpkin puree, pumpkin pie spice, maple syrup

Instructions: Mix waffle batter with pumpkin puree and pumpkin pie spice until well combined. Cook in a preheated waffle iron according to manufacturer's instructions. Serve with maple syrup.

Cooking Time: Varies based on waffle iron

Other: Perfect for fall mornings or any time of year.

✢ Ricotta and Berry Stuffed French Toast

Ingredients: Bread slices, ricotta cheese, mixed berries, eggs, milk, vanilla extract, maple syrup

Instructions: Spread ricotta cheese onto bread slices and top with mixed berries. Sandwich bread slices together to form French toast. Whisk together eggs, milk, and vanilla extract. Dip stuffed French toast into egg mixture and air fry at 350°F for 6-8 minutes, until golden and crispy.

Cooking Time: 6-8 minutes

Other: Serve with maple syrup for a decadent breakfast treat.

✤ Breakfast Sausage Patties

Ingredients: Ground pork or turkey, maple syrup, sage, thyme, salt, pepper

Instructions: Mix ground pork or turkey with maple syrup, sage, thyme, salt, and pepper until well combined. Shape mixture into patties. Air fry at 375°F for 10-12 minutes, flipping halfway through, until cooked through.

Cooking Time: 10-12 minutes

Other: Serve with eggs and toast for a classic breakfast combo.

✤ Quinoa Breakfast Bowl

Ingredients: Cooked quinoa, Greek yogurt, fresh berries, honey, chopped nuts

Instructions: Spoon cooked quinoa into serving bowls. Top with Greek yogurt, fresh berries, honey, and chopped nuts. Serve immediately.

Cooking Time: No cooking required

Other: Customize with your favorite toppings for a nutritious breakfast option.

✦ Breakfast BLT Sandwich

Ingredients: Bread slices, cooked bacon, lettuce, tomato slices, avocado, mayonnaise

Instructions: Assemble sandwiches with bread slices, cooked bacon, lettuce, tomato slices, and avocado. Spread mayonnaise on bread slices. Wrap sandwiches in foil and air fry at 350°F for 3-5 minutes, until heated through.

Cooking Time: 3-5 minutes

Other: A satisfying twist on the classic BLT.

✦ Almond Butter Banana Smoothie

Ingredients: Ripe bananas, almond butter, almond milk, honey, ice cubes

Instructions: Blend ripe bananas, almond butter, almond milk, honey, and ice cubes until smooth and creamy. Serve immediately.

Cooking Time: No cooking required

Other: A quick and nourishing breakfast option.

✦ Breakfast Fruit Salad

Ingredients: Assorted fresh fruits (such as berries, melon, pineapple, grapes), Greek yogurt, honey, chopped mint

Instructions: Chop fresh fruits into bite-sized pieces and toss together in a bowl. Serve with Greek yogurt drizzled with honey and garnished with chopped mint.

Cooking Time: No cooking required

Other: A refreshing and healthy start to the day.

LUNCH

QUICK AND EASY LUNCH RECIPES SUITABLE FOR BUSY SCHEDULES

⊹ Chicken Caesar Salad Wraps

Ingredients: Grilled chicken breast, romaine lettuce, Caesar dressing, Parmesan cheese, whole wheat wraps

Instructions: Toss grilled chicken with Caesar dressing, lettuce, and cheese. Divide mixture among wraps, roll up, and enjoy!

Cooking Time: 15 minutes

⊹ Caprese Sandwich

Ingredients: Fresh mozzarella, ripe tomatoes, basil leaves, balsamic glaze, ciabatta bread

Instructions: Layer mozzarella, tomato, and basil on ciabatta bread. Drizzle with balsamic glaze and serve.

Cooking Time: 10 minutes

✦ Greek Chicken Pita Pockets

Ingredients: Grilled chicken strips, diced cucumber, cherry tomatoes, feta cheese, tzatziki sauce, whole wheat pita pockets

Instructions: Fill pita pockets with chicken, cucumber, tomatoes, feta, and tzatziki sauce.

Cooking Time: 15 minutes

✦ Avocado Toast with Smoked Salmon

Ingredients: Whole grain bread, ripe avocado, smoked salmon, cherry tomatoes, lemon juice

Instructions: Toast bread, spread avocado, top with smoked salmon and tomatoes. Drizzle with lemon juice.

Cooking Time: 10 minutes

✤ Mediterranean Quinoa Salad

Ingredients: Cooked quinoa, cherry tomatoes, cucumber, Kalamata olives, feta cheese, lemon vinaigrette

Instructions: Toss quinoa with tomatoes, cucumber, olives, and feta. Drizzle with lemon vinaigrette.

Cooking Time: 20 minutes

✤ Turkey and Hummus Wrap

Ingredients: Sliced turkey breast, hummus, baby spinach, whole wheat tortilla

Instructions: Spread hummus on tortilla, layer with turkey and spinach. Roll up and slice.

Cooking Time: 10 minutes

✤ Vegetable Stir-Fry

Ingredients: Mixed vegetables (bell peppers, broccoli, carrots), tofu or chicken, soy sauce, garlic, ginger, sesame oil

Instructions: Stir-fry vegetables and protein in sesame oil with garlic and ginger. Add soy sauce and serve.

Cooking Time: 20 minutes

⚜ BLT Salad

Ingredients: Mixed greens, crispy bacon, cherry tomatoes, avocado, ranch dressing

Instructions: Toss greens with bacon, tomatoes, avocado, and ranch dressing.

Cooking Time: 15 minutes

⚜ Tuna Salad Lettuce Wraps

Ingredients: Canned tuna, diced celery, red onion, mayonnaise, Dijon mustard, lettuce leaves

Instructions: Mix tuna with celery, onion, mayo, and mustard. Spoon onto lettuce leaves and wrap.

Cooking Time: 10 minutes

⁜ Turkey and Cranberry Panini

Ingredients: Sliced turkey breast, cranberry sauce, Swiss cheese, whole grain bread

Instructions: Layer turkey, cranberry sauce, and Swiss cheese between bread slices. Grill until golden brown.

Cooking Time: 15 minutes

⁜ Asian Chicken Salad

Ingredients: Shredded chicken breast, mixed greens, mandarin oranges, sliced almonds, Asian sesame dressing

Instructions: Toss chicken, greens, oranges, and almonds with dressing. Serve.

Cooking Time: 15 minutes

⁜ Veggie Quesadillas

Ingredients: Tortillas, black beans, bell peppers, onions, shredded cheese, salsa

Instructions: Layer beans, vegetables, and cheese on tortillas. Cook until cheese melts. Serve with salsa.

Cooking Time: 15 minutes

✤ Egg Salad Sandwich

Ingredients: Hard-boiled eggs, mayonnaise, Dijon mustard, green onions, lettuce, whole grain bread

Instructions: Mash eggs with mayo, mustard, and onions. Spread on bread, add lettuce, and assemble sandwich.

Cooking Time: 20 minutes

✤ Shrimp and Avocado Salad

Ingredients: Cooked shrimp, avocado, cherry tomatoes, cucumber, mixed greens, lemon vinaigrette

Instructions: Toss shrimp, avocado, tomatoes, and cucumber with mixed greens and dressing.

Cooking Time: 15 minutes

✢ Mushroom and Spinach Quesadillas

Ingredients: Tortillas, sautéed mushrooms, spinach, shredded cheese, salsa

Instructions: Layer mushrooms, spinach, and cheese on tortillas. Cook until cheese melts. Serve with salsa.

Cooking Time: 15 minutes

✢ Thai Peanut Chicken Lettuce Wraps

Ingredients: Shredded chicken, shredded carrots, sliced bell peppers, peanuts, Thai peanut sauce, lettuce leaves

Instructions: Fill lettuce leaves with chicken, carrots, peppers, peanuts, and sauce. Wrap and enjoy.

Cooking Time: 15 minutes

✤ Tomato Basil Mozzarella Panini

Ingredients: Sliced tomatoes, fresh mozzarella, basil leaves, pesto, ciabatta bread

Instructions: Layer tomatoes, mozzarella, and basil on ciabatta. Spread pesto on bread and grill until cheese melts.

Cooking Time: 15 minutes

✤ Chicken Caesar Salad

Ingredients: Grilled chicken breast, romaine lettuce, Caesar dressing, croutons, Parmesan cheese

Instructions: Toss chicken, lettuce, dressing, and croutons. Top with Parmesan cheese and serve.

Cooking Time: 15 minutes

✤ Southwest Chicken Wrap

Ingredients: Grilled chicken strips, black beans, corn, diced tomatoes, shredded cheese, chipotle mayo, whole wheat tortilla

Instructions: Fill tortilla with chicken, beans, corn, tomatoes, cheese, and mayo. Roll up and enjoy.

Cooking Time: 15 minutes

✦ Eggplant Parmesan Sandwich

Ingredients: Breaded and fried eggplant slices, marinara sauce, mozzarella cheese, whole grain bread

Instructions: Layer eggplant, sauce, and cheese on bread. Grill until cheese melts.

Cooking Time: 20 minutes

✦ Taco Salad

Ingredients: Ground beef or turkey, lettuce, diced tomatoes, shredded cheese, black beans, salsa, tortilla chips

Instructions: Cook meat, toss with lettuce, tomatoes, cheese, beans, and salsa. Serve with tortilla chips.

Cooking Time: 20 minutes

✛ Cucumber Avocado Roll-Ups

Ingredients: Sliced cucumber, mashed avocado, smoked salmon or turkey, alfalfa sprouts

Instructions: Spread avocado on cucumber slices, top with salmon or turkey and sprouts. Roll up and serve.

Cooking Time: 10 minutes

✛ Mediterranean Veggie Wraps

Ingredients: Hummus, roasted red peppers, cucumber slices, Kalamata olives, feta cheese, and whole wheat wraps

Instructions: Spread hummus on wraps, add peppers, cucumber, olives, and feta. Roll up and enjoy.

Cooking Time: 10 minutes

✦ Spinach and Feta Stuffed Portobello Mushrooms

Ingredients: Portobello mushrooms, sautéed spinach, crumbled feta cheese, garlic, olive oil

Instructions: Stuff mushrooms with spinach and feta mixture. Drizzle with olive oil and bake until tender.

Cooking Time: 20 minutes

✦ Italian Sub Salad

Ingredients: Mixed greens, salami, pepperoni slices, provolone cheese, cherry tomatoes, Italian dressing

Instructions: Toss greens with salami, pepperoni, cheese, tomatoes, and dressing. Serve.

Cooking Time: 15 minutes

57 | FRIED TO PERFECTION

DINNER

FLAVORFUL DINNER RECIPES FOR THE WHOLE FAMILY

✦ Crispy Coconut Shrimp

Ingredients: Shrimp, coconut flakes, flour, eggs, salt, pepper

Instructions: Coat shrimp in flour, dip in beaten eggs, then coat with coconut flakes. Air fry at 380°F for 8-10 minutes, flipping halfway.

✦ BBQ Chicken Wings

Ingredients: Chicken wings, BBQ sauce, salt, pepper

Instructions: Toss chicken wings in BBQ sauce, season with salt and pepper. Air fry at 400°F for 25-30 minutes, flipping halfway.

⚜ Garlic Parmesan Cauliflower Bites

Ingredients: Cauliflower florets, Parmesan cheese, garlic powder, olive oil, salt, pepper

Instructions: Toss cauliflower in olive oil, garlic powder, and Parmesan cheese. Air fry at 375°F for 15-18 minutes, shaking halfway.

⚜ Crispy Breaded Pork Chops

Ingredients: Pork chops, breadcrumbs, Parmesan cheese, Italian seasoning, salt, pepper

Instructions: Coat pork chops in breadcrumb mixture. Air fry at 375°F for 12-15 minutes, flipping halfway.

⚜ Teriyaki Salmon

Ingredients: Salmon fillets, teriyaki sauce, sesame seeds, green onions

Instructions: Marinate salmon in teriyaki sauce, sprinkle with sesame seeds and green onions. Air fry at 360°F for 10-12 minutes.

✣ Stuffed Bell Peppers

Ingredients: Bell peppers, ground beef, rice, onion, garlic, tomato sauce, cheese

Instructions: Cook ground beef, rice, onion, and garlic. Stuff mixture into bell peppers, top with cheese. Air fry at 370°F for 20-25 minutes.

✣ Crispy Chicken Parmesan

Ingredients: Chicken breasts, breadcrumbs, Parmesan cheese, marinara sauce, mozzarella cheese

Instructions: Coat chicken in breadcrumb mixture, top with marinara and mozzarella. Air fry at 380°F for 18-20 minutes.

✣ Lemon Herb Roasted Chicken

Ingredients: Chicken thighs, lemon juice, olive oil, garlic, rosemary, thyme, salt, pepper

Instructions: Marinate chicken in lemon juice, olive oil, garlic, and herbs. Air fry at 375°F for 25-30 minutes.

✤ Spicy Cajun Shrimp

Ingredients: Shrimp, Cajun seasoning, olive oil, lemon juice

Instructions: Toss shrimp in Cajun seasoning, olive oil, and lemon juice. Air fry at 400°F for 5-7 minutes.

✤ Honey Mustard Glazed Pork Tenderloin

Ingredients: Pork tenderloin, honey, Dijon mustard, garlic powder, salt, pepper

Instructions: Mix honey, mustard, and garlic powder. Brush over pork tenderloin. Air fry at 375°F for 20-25 minutes.

✤ Mediterranean Stuffed Chicken

Ingredients: Chicken breasts, spinach, feta cheese, sun-dried tomatoes, garlic, Italian seasoning

Instructions: Stuff chicken with spinach, feta, tomatoes, and garlic. Air fry at 375°F for 20-25 minutes.

✦ Lemon Pepper Wings

Ingredients: Chicken wings, lemon pepper seasoning, olive oil

Instructions: Toss wings in seasoning and oil. Air fry at 380°F for 25-30 minutes, flipping halfway.

✦ Sesame Ginger Tofu

Ingredients: Tofu, soy sauce, sesame oil, ginger, garlic, green onions, sesame seeds

Instructions: Marinate tofu in soy sauce, sesame oil, ginger, and garlic. Air fry at 370°F for 15-20 minutes, flipping halfway.

✦ Beef and Broccoli Stir-Fry

Ingredients: Beef sirloin, broccoli florets, soy sauce, garlic, ginger, brown sugar, cornstarch

Instructions: Stir-fry beef and broccoli with sauce. Air fry at 375°F for 8-10 minutes.

⚜ Crispy Buffalo Cauliflower

Ingredients: Cauliflower florets, buffalo sauce, flour, garlic powder, butter

Instructions: Toss cauliflower in flour, garlic powder, and butter. Air fry at 380°F for 12-15 minutes, tossing halfway.

⚜ Southwest Stuffed Peppers

Ingredients: Bell peppers, ground turkey, black beans, corn, salsa, cheese

Instructions: Cook turkey with beans, corn, and salsa. Stuff into peppers, top with cheese. Air fry at 370°F for 20-25 minutes.

⚜ Lemon Herb Salmon

Ingredients: Salmon fillets, lemon zest, garlic, parsley, olive oil, salt, pepper

Instructions: Coat salmon with lemon zest, garlic, parsley, and oil. Air fry at 360°F for 10-12 minutes.

✤ Crispy Coconut Tofu

Ingredients: Tofu, coconut flakes, flour, eggs, salt, pepper

Instructions: Coat tofu in flour, dip in beaten eggs, then coat with coconut flakes. Air fry at 380°F for 10-12 minutes, flipping halfway.

✤ Honey Sriracha Chicken

Ingredients: Chicken thighs, honey, Sriracha sauce, soy sauce, garlic, ginger

Instructions: Marinate chicken in honey, Sriracha, soy sauce, garlic, and ginger. Air fry at 375°F for 20-25 minutes.

✤ Cajun Shrimp and Sausage

Ingredients: Shrimp, sausage, Cajun seasoning, bell peppers, onion

Instructions: Toss shrimp, sausage, and vegetables in Cajun seasoning. Air fry at 380°F for 10-12 minutes.

⚜ Parmesan Crusted Pork Chops

Ingredients: Pork chops, Parmesan cheese, breadcrumbs, garlic powder, Italian seasoning

Instructions: Coat pork chops in Parmesan, breadcrumbs, and seasoning. Air fry at 375°F for 12-15 minutes, flipping halfway.

⚜ Balsamic Glazed Chicken

Ingredients: Chicken breasts, balsamic vinegar, honey, garlic, rosemary, thyme

Instructions: Marinate chicken in balsamic, honey, garlic, and herbs. Air fry at 375°F for 20-25 minutes.

⚜ Soy Ginger Glazed Salmon

Ingredients: Salmon fillets, soy sauce, ginger, garlic, honey, green onions

Instructions: Marinate salmon in soy sauce, ginger, garlic, and honey. Air fry at 360°F for 10-12 minutes.

✤ Crispy Ranch Chicken Tenders

Ingredients: Chicken tenders, ranch seasoning, flour, eggs, breadcrumbs

Instructions: Coat chicken in ranch seasoning, flour, eggs, and breadcrumbs. Air fry at 380°F for 12-15 minutes, flipping halfway.

✤ Mushroom and Spinach Stuffed Chicken

Ingredients: Chicken breasts, mushrooms, spinach, garlic, cream cheese, Parmesan cheese

Instructions: Stuff chicken with mushroom, spinach, garlic, cream cheese, and Parmesan. Air fry at 375°F for 20-25 minutes.

SNACKS

SNACK RECIPES PERFECT FOR ANY TIME OF THE DAY

✢ Crispy Kale Chips

Ingredients: Kale leaves, olive oil, salt, optional seasonings (such as garlic powder or nutritional yeast)

Instructions: Preheat the air fryer to 350°F (180°C). Tear the kale leaves into bite-sized pieces and toss with olive oil, salt, and any desired seasonings. Arrange the kale pieces in a single layer in the air fryer basket. Cook for 5-7 minutes, shaking the basket halfway through, until the kale is crispy.

Cooking Time: 5-7 minutes

✢ Buffalo Cauliflower Bites

Ingredients: Cauliflower florets, buffalo sauce, olive oil, garlic powder, salt

Instructions: Preheat the air fryer to 375°F (190°C). Toss cauliflower florets with buffalo sauce, olive oil, garlic powder, and salt until evenly coated. Arrange the cauliflower in a single layer in the air fryer basket. Cook for 15-20 minutes, shaking the basket halfway through, until the cauliflower is crispy and golden.

Cooking Time: 15-20 minutes

✢ Homemade Potato Chips

Ingredients: Potatoes, olive oil, salt, optional seasonings (such as paprika or rosemary)

Instructions: Thinly slice potatoes using a mandoline or sharp knife. Soak the potato slices in cold water for 30 minutes, then pat dry with paper towels. Toss the potato slices with olive oil, salt, and any desired seasonings. Arrange the potato slices in a single layer in the air fryer basket. Cook for 10-15 minutes, flipping halfway through, until the chips are crispy and golden.

Cooking Time: 10-15 minutes

✤ Garlic Parmesan Zucchini Fries

Ingredients: Zucchini, grated Parmesan cheese, garlic powder, Italian seasoning, salt, egg, breadcrumbs

Instructions: Preheat the air fryer to 400°F (200°C). Cut the zucchini into fries-like shapes. In one bowl, whisk together egg. In another bowl, mix breadcrumbs, grated Parmesan cheese, garlic powder, Italian seasoning, and salt. Dip each zucchini fry into the egg, then coat with the breadcrumb mixture. Arrange the coated fries in a single layer in the air fryer basket. Cook for 10-12 minutes, flipping halfway through, until the fries are golden and crispy.

Cooking Time: 10-12 minutes

✤ Crispy Chickpeas

Ingredients: Canned chickpeas, olive oil, salt, optional seasonings (such as cumin, paprika, or chili powder)

Instructions: Preheat the air fryer to 400°F (200°C). Rinse and drain the chickpeas, then pat dry with paper towels. Toss the chickpeas with olive oil, salt, and any desired seasonings. Arrange the chickpeas in a single layer in the air fryer basket. Cook for 15-20 minutes, shaking the basket halfway through, until the chickpeas are crispy and golden.

Cooking Time: 15-20 minutes

✚ Zucchini Parmesan Chips

Ingredients: Zucchini, grated Parmesan cheese, Italian seasoning, garlic powder, salt, egg

Instructions: Preheat the air fryer to 400°F (200°C). Slice the zucchini into thin rounds. In one bowl, whisk together egg. In another bowl, mix grated Parmesan cheese, Italian seasoning, garlic powder, and salt. Dip each zucchini round into the egg, then coat with the Parmesan mixture. Arrange the coated zucchini rounds in a single layer in the air fryer basket. Cook for 8-10 minutes, flipping halfway through, until the chips are crispy and golden.

Cooking Time: 8-10 minutes

⁕ Apple Cinnamon Chips

Ingredients: Apples, cinnamon, sugar (optional)

Instructions: Preheat the air fryer to 350°F (180°C). Thinly slice apples using a mandoline or sharp knife, removing the seeds. Toss the apple slices with cinnamon and sugar (if using). Arrange the apple slices in a single layer in the air fryer basket. Cook for 8-10 minutes, flipping halfway through, until the chips are crispy and lightly golden.

Cooking Time: 8-10 minutes

⁕ Crispy Mozzarella Sticks

Ingredients: Mozzarella string cheese, egg, breadcrumbs, Italian seasoning, marinara sauce (for dipping)

Instructions: Preheat the air fryer to 390°F (200°C). Cut the mozzarella sticks in half. In one bowl, whisk together egg. In another bowl, mix breadcrumbs and Italian seasoning. Dip each mozzarella stick half into the egg, then coat with the breadcrumb mixture. Arrange the coated mozzarella sticks in a single layer in the air fryer basket. Cook for 6-8 minutes, until the sticks are crispy and golden.

Cooking Time: 6-8 minutes

⊹ Cinnamon Sugar Donut Holes

Ingredients: Canned biscuit dough, melted butter, cinnamon, sugar

Instructions: Preheat the air fryer to 350°F (180°C). Cut each biscuit dough into quarters. In a bowl, mix melted butter, cinnamon, and sugar. Toss the biscuit quarters in the cinnamon sugar mixture until evenly coated. Arrange the coated biscuit quarters in a single layer in the air fryer basket. Cook for 5-6 minutes, shaking the basket halfway through, until the donut holes are golden and cooked through.

Cooking Time: 5-6 minutes

✦ Coconut Shrimp

Ingredients: Large shrimp, shredded coconut, egg, breadcrumbs, salt, sweet chili sauce (for dipping)

Instructions: Preheat the air fryer to 375°F (190°C). Peel and devein the shrimp, leaving the tails intact. In one bowl, whisk the egg. In another bowl, mix shredded coconut, breadcrumbs, and salt. Dip each shrimp into the egg, then coat with the coconut breadcrumb mixture. Arrange the coated shrimp in a single layer in the air fryer basket. Cook for 8-10 minutes, flipping halfway through, until the shrimp are golden and crispy.

Cooking Time: 8-10 minutes

✦ Crispy Brussels Sprouts

Ingredients: Brussels sprouts, olive oil, balsamic vinegar, salt, pepper, grated Parmesan cheese (optional)

Instructions: Preheat the air fryer to 375°F (190°C). Trim the stems and halve the Brussels sprouts. In a bowl, toss Brussels sprouts with olive oil, balsamic vinegar, salt, and pepper until evenly coated. Arrange the Brussels sprouts in a single layer in the air fryer basket. Cook for 15-20 minutes, shaking the basket halfway through, until the Brussels sprouts are crispy and caramelized. Sprinkle with grated Parmesan cheese, if desired, before serving.

Cooking Time: 15-20 minutes

✤ Mozzarella Stuffed Meatballs

Ingredients: Ground beef or turkey, Italian seasoning, garlic powder, onion powder, salt, pepper, mozzarella cheese cubes, marinara sauce (for dipping)

Instructions: Preheat the air fryer to 375°F (190°C). In a bowl, mix ground meat with Italian seasoning, garlic powder, onion powder, salt, and pepper until well combined. Take a small portion of the meat mixture and flatten it in the palm of your hand. Place a mozzarella cheese cube in the center and roll the meat mixture around it to form a meatball. Repeat with the remaining meat mixture and cheese cubes. Arrange the meatballs in a single layer in the air fryer basket. Cook for 12-15 minutes, until the meatballs are cooked through and golden brown. Serve with marinara sauce for dipping.

Cooking Time: 12-15 minutes

✚ Crispy Chicken Wings

Ingredients: Chicken wings, baking powder, salt, pepper, garlic powder, barbecue sauce (for dipping)

Instructions: Preheat the air fryer to 400°F (200°C). Pat the chicken wings dry with paper towels. In a bowl, toss the chicken wings with baking powder, salt, pepper, and garlic powder until evenly coated. Arrange the chicken wings in a single layer in the air fryer basket. Cook for 25-30 minutes, shaking the basket halfway through, until the wings are crispy and golden brown. Serve with barbecue sauce for dipping.

Cooking Time: 25-30 minutes

✠ Jalapeño Poppers

Ingredients: Jalapeño peppers, cream cheese, shredded cheddar cheese, bacon (optional), breadcrumbs

Instructions: Preheat the air fryer to 375°F (190°C). Cut jalapeño peppers in half lengthwise and remove the seeds and membranes. In a bowl, mix cream cheese and shredded cheddar cheese until well combined. If using bacon, cook it until crispy and crumble it into the cheese mixture. Spoon the cheese mixture into the jalapeño halves. Sprinkle breadcrumbs on top. Arrange the jalapeño poppers in a single layer in the air fryer basket. Cook for 10-12 minutes, until the cheese is bubbly and the jalapeños are tender. Serve hot.

Cooking Time: 10-12 minutes

✠ Homemade Tortilla Chips

Ingredients: Corn tortillas, olive oil, salt, lime wedges (for serving)

Instructions: Preheat the air fryer to 375°F (190°C). Cut corn tortillas into wedges or strips. Brush both sides of the tortilla wedges lightly with olive oil and sprinkle with salt. Arrange the tortilla wedges in a single layer in the air fryer basket. Cook for 6-8 minutes, flipping halfway through, until the chips are golden and crispy. Serve with lime wedges and your favorite salsa or guacamole.

Cooking Time: 6-8 minutes

✢ Crispy Tofu Bites

Ingredients: Extra-firm tofu, soy sauce, sesame oil, cornstarch, garlic powder, ginger powder, green onions (for garnish)

Instructions: Preheat the air fryer to 375°F (190°C). Cut tofu into bite-sized cubes. In a bowl, mix soy sauce, sesame oil, cornstarch, garlic powder, and ginger powder until smooth. Toss the tofu cubes in the marinade until evenly coated. Arrange the tofu cubes in a single layer in the air fryer basket. Cook for 15-20 minutes, shaking the basket halfway through, until the tofu is crispy and golden. Garnish with sliced green onions before serving.

Cooking Time: 15-20 minutes

⁕ Cajun Sweet Potato Fries

Ingredients: Sweet potatoes, olive oil, Cajun seasoning, salt

Instructions: Preheat the air fryer to 400°F (200°C). Cut sweet potatoes into fries-like shapes. In a bowl, toss the sweet potato fries with olive oil, Cajun seasoning, and salt until evenly coated. Arrange the sweet potato fries in a single layer in the air fryer basket. Cook for 15-20 minutes, shaking the basket halfway through, until the fries are crispy and lightly browned. Serve hot.

Cooking Time: 15-20 minutes

⁕ Stuffed Mushrooms

Ingredients: Large mushrooms, cream cheese, garlic, breadcrumbs, grated Parmesan cheese, parsley (for garnish)

Instructions: Preheat the air fryer to 375°F (190°C). Remove the stems from the mushrooms and hollow out the caps slightly. In a bowl, mix cream cheese, minced garlic, breadcrumbs, and grated Parmesan cheese until well combined. Spoon the cream cheese mixture into the mushroom caps. Arrange the stuffed mushrooms in a single layer in the air fryer basket. Cook for 10-12 minutes, until the mushrooms are tender and the filling is golden brown. Garnish with chopped parsley before serving.

Cooking Time: 10-12 minutes

⊕ Crispy Onion Rings

Ingredients: Yellow onions, buttermilk, flour, cornmeal, salt, pepper, paprika, garlic powder, cooking spray

Instructions: Preheat the air fryer to 375°F (190°C). Cut onions into thick rings and separate the rings. Soak the onion rings in buttermilk for

30 minutes. In a bowl, mix flour, cornmeal, salt, pepper, paprika, and garlic powder. Dredge the onion rings in the flour mixture, shaking off any excess. Spray the onion rings lightly with cooking spray. Arrange the onion rings in a single layer in the air fryer basket. Cook for 10-12 minutes, flipping halfway through, until the onion rings are crispy and golden brown.

Cooking Time: 10-12 minutes

✢ Cinnamon Apple Chips

Ingredients: Apples, cinnamon, sugar (optional)

Instructions: Preheat the air fryer to 350°F (180°C). Thinly slice apples using a mandoline or sharp knife, removing the seeds. Toss the apple slices with cinnamon and sugar (if using). Arrange the apple slices in a single layer in the air fryer basket. Cook for 8-10 minutes, flipping halfway through, until the chips are crispy and lightly golden.

Cooking Time: 8-10 minutes

✣ Crispy Avocado Fries

Ingredients: Avocados, flour, eggs, breadcrumbs, salt, lime wedges (for serving)

Instructions: Preheat the air fryer to 375°F (190°C). Cut avocados into thick slices or wedges. In one bowl, place flour. In another bowl, beat eggs. In a third bowl, place breadcrumbs mixed with salt. Dredge each avocado slice in flour, then dip in egg, and coat with breadcrumbs. Arrange the coated avocado slices in a single layer in the air fryer basket. Cook for 10-12 minutes, flipping halfway through, until the avocado fries are golden and crispy. Serve with lime wedges for squeezing over the fries.

Cooking Time: 10-12 minutes

✣ Crispy Pickles

Ingredients: Pickle slices, flour, eggs, breadcrumbs, salt, pepper, ranch dressing (for dipping)

Instructions: Preheat the air fryer to 375°F (190°C). Pat the pickle slices dry with paper towels. In one bowl, place flour. In another bowl, beat eggs. In a third bowl, place breadcrumbs mixed with salt and pepper. Dredge each pickle slice in flour, then dip in egg, and coat with breadcrumbs. Arrange the coated pickle slices in a single layer in the air fryer basket. Cook for 8-10 minutes, flipping halfway through, until the pickles are golden and crispy. Serve with ranch dressing for dipping.

Cooking Time: 8-10 minutes

⊥ Crispy Asparagus Spears

Ingredients: Asparagus spears, olive oil, grated Parmesan cheese, breadcrumbs, salt, pepper, lemon wedges (for serving)

Instructions: Preheat the air fryer to 400°F (200°C). Trim the tough ends of the asparagus spears. Toss the asparagus spears with olive oil, grated Parmesan cheese, breadcrumbs, salt, and pepper until evenly coated. Arrange the asparagus spears in a single layer in the air fryer basket. Cook for 8-10 minutes, shaking the basket halfway through, until the asparagus is crispy and tender. Serve with lemon wedges for squeezing over the asparagus.

Cooking Time: 8-10 minutes

⁺ Crispy Green Bean Fries

Ingredients: Green beans, flour, eggs, breadcrumbs, Parmesan cheese, garlic powder, salt, marinara sauce (for dipping)

Instructions: Preheat the air fryer to 375°F (190°C). Trim the ends of the green beans. In one bowl, place flour. In another bowl, beat eggs. In a third bowl, place breadcrumbs mixed with Parmesan cheese, garlic powder, and salt. Dredge each green bean in flour, then dip in egg, and coat with breadcrumb mixture. Arrange the coated green beans in a single layer in the air fryer basket. Cook for 10-12 minutes, until the green beans are golden and crispy. Serve with marinara sauce for dipping.

Cooking Time: 10-12 minutes

✢ Honey Sriracha Chicken Wings

Ingredients: Chicken wings, honey, Sriracha sauce, soy sauce, garlic powder, salt, sesame seeds (for garnish)

Instructions: Preheat the air fryer to 380°F (190°C). Pat the chicken wings dry with paper towels. In a bowl, mix honey, Sriracha sauce, soy sauce, garlic powder, and salt. Toss the chicken wings in the sauce until evenly coated. Arrange the chicken wings in a single layer in the air fryer basket. Cook for 25-30 minutes, shaking the basket halfway through, until the wings are crispy and cooked through. Sprinkle with sesame seeds before serving.

Cooking Time: 25-30 minutes

DESSERTS / SMOOTHIES

INDULGENT DESSERTS AND REFRESHING SMOOTHIE RECIPES MADE HEALTHIER WITH THE AIR FRYER

INDULGENT DESSERTS:

- **Air-Fried Chocolate Lava Cake**

Ingredients: Flour, sugar, cocoa powder, eggs, butter, chocolate chips

Instructions: Mix ingredients, pour into ramekins, air fry at 350°F for 8-10 minutes.

Serve with a dusting of powdered sugar and a scoop of vanilla ice cream.

⊕ Cinnamon Sugar Donut Holes

Ingredients: Biscuit dough, cinnamon, sugar, melted butter

Instructions: Cut dough into small balls, coat in cinnamon sugar mixture, air fry at 350°F for 5-7 minutes.

Enjoy warm with a cup of coffee.

⊕ Apple Pie Turnovers

Ingredients: Pie crust, apples, sugar, cinnamon, nutmeg, butter

Instructions: Fill pie crust with apple mixture, seal edges, air fry at 375°F for 10-12 minutes.

Serve with a drizzle of caramel sauce.

⊕ Banana Nutella Empanadas

Ingredients: Flour tortillas, bananas, Nutella, chopped hazelnuts

Instructions: Fill tortillas with banana slices and Nutella, fold into empanadas, air fry at 370°F for 8-10 minutes.

Sprinkle with chopped hazelnuts before serving.

✤ Air-Fried Cheesecake Stuffed Strawberries

Ingredients: Strawberries, cream cheese, powdered sugar, vanilla extract, graham cracker crumbs

Instructions: Mix cream cheese, sugar, and vanilla, stuff strawberries, roll in graham cracker crumbs, air fry at 350°F for 5-6 minutes.

Garnish with whipped cream and a mint leaf.

✤ Churro Bites with Chocolate Sauce

Ingredients: Puff pastry, sugar, cinnamon, chocolate chips, heavy cream

Instructions: Cut puff pastry into small squares, coat in cinnamon sugar mixture, air fry at 375°F for 6-8 minutes.

Melt chocolate chips and cream for dipping sauce.

✣ Air-Fried S'mores

Ingredients: Graham crackers, marshmallows, chocolate squares

Instructions: Assemble s'mores, air fry at 375°F for 3-4 minutes.

Serve warm and gooey.

✣ Peach Cobbler

Ingredients: Peaches, sugar, flour, oats, butter, cinnamon

Instructions: Mix peaches with sugar, top with oat mixture, air fry at 370°F for 12-15 minutes.

Serve with a scoop of vanilla ice cream.

✣ Air-Fried Strawberry Shortcake

Ingredients: Biscuits, strawberries, sugar, whipped cream

Instructions: Slice biscuits, layer with strawberries and sugar, air fry at 350°F for 6-8 minutes.

Top with whipped cream before serving.

✦ Crispy Coconut Shrimp

Ingredients: Shrimp, flour, eggs, shredded coconut, panko breadcrumbs

Instructions: Coat shrimp in flour, dip in beaten eggs, coat with coconut and breadcrumbs, air fry at 375°F for 8-10 minutes.

Serve with sweet chili dipping sauce.

✦ Air-Fried Peanut Butter Banana Spring Rolls

Ingredients: Spring roll wrappers, bananas, peanut butter, chocolate chips

Instructions: Fill wrappers with banana slices, peanut butter, and chocolate chips, roll up, air fry at 370°F for 6-8 minutes.

Serve with a drizzle of honey.

✜ Lemon Blueberry Bread Pudding

Ingredients: Bread cubes, blueberries, eggs, milk, sugar, lemon zest

Instructions: Mix ingredients, pour into greased pan, air fry at 350°F for 15-18 minutes.

Serve warm with a dusting of powdered sugar.

REFRESHING SMOOTHIES:

✜ Tropical Paradise Smoothie

Ingredients: Pineapple, mango, banana, coconut water, ice

Instructions: Blend all ingredients until smooth.

✜ Berry Blast Smoothie

Ingredients: Mixed berries, Greek yogurt, honey, almond milk, ice

Instructions: Blend all ingredients until smooth.

⁜ Green Goddess Smoothie

Ingredients: Spinach, kale, banana, avocado, almond milk, honey, ice

Instructions: Blend all ingredients until smooth.

⁜ Peachy Keen Smoothie

Ingredients: Peaches, Greek yogurt, orange juice, honey, ice

Instructions: Blend all ingredients until smooth.

⁜ Chocolate Banana Smoothie

Ingredients: Banana, cocoa powder, almond milk, honey, ice

Instructions: Blend all ingredients until smooth.

⁜ Minty Watermelon Smoothie

Ingredients: Watermelon, mint leaves, lime juice, honey, ice

Instructions: Blend all ingredients until smooth.

⁜ Pina Colada Smoothie

Ingredients: Pineapple, coconut milk, Greek yogurt, honey, ice

Instructions: Blend all ingredients until smooth.

⁜ Strawberry Kiwi Smoothie

Ingredients: Strawberries, kiwi, orange juice, Greek yogurt, honey, ice

Instructions: Blend all ingredients until smooth.

⁜ Mango Tango Smoothie

Ingredients: Mango, banana, orange juice, Greek yogurt, honey, ice

Instructions: Blend all ingredients until smooth.

⁜ Blueberry Avocado Smoothie

Ingredients: Blueberries, avocado, spinach, almond milk, honey, ice

Instructions: Blend all ingredients until smooth.

❖ Raspberry Coconut Smoothie

Ingredients: Raspberries, coconut milk, Greek yogurt, honey, ice

Instructions: Blend all ingredients until smooth.

❖ Orange Creamsicle Smoothie

Ingredients: Oranges, Greek yogurt, vanilla extract, honey, ice

Instructions: Blend all ingredients until smooth.

❖ Cherry Almond Smoothie

Ingredients: Cherries, almond milk, Greek yogurt, honey, ice

Instructions: Blend all ingredients until smooth.

MEAL PLAN

Finding time to prepare healthy meals in the busy rhythm of modern life can often seem like a daunting task. That's where our meal plan comes in - a carefully curated selection of breakfasts, lunches and dinners designed to simplify your week and delight your taste buds. Each dish is created with the versatility and convenience of deep fryer cooking in mind, making it easier than ever to enjoy delicious home-cooked meals without sacrificing taste or nutrition.

Now let's dive into our meal plan and explore the delicious options that await:

SAMPLE MEAL PLANS:

Breakfast:

Start your day right with a satisfying breakfast that is both tasty and nutritious. From sweet to savory, these breakfast recipes are sure to please even the pickiest of palates. Indulge in crunchy cinnamon French toast sticks or fuel up with protein-packed breakfast burritos, all cooked to perfection in your trusty deep fryer.

Lunch:

Say goodbye to boring lunches at the table and welcome delicious lunches that will keep you energized and satisfied all day long. Whether you're craving a crunchy salad, a hearty wrap or a comforting sandwich, our lunch options will satisfy you. With bold flavors and healthy ingredients, these recipes are a great way to break up a busy day.

Dinner:

End your day with a sensational dinner that will calm and satisfy you. From crispy coconut shrimp to juicy BBQ chicken drumsticks, these dinner recipes are sure to please the whole family. And with the convenience of deep fryer cooking, you can enjoy gourmet meals without spending hours in the kitchen.

AIR FRYER MEAL PREP TIPS TO SAVE TIME DURING THE WEEK:

Now that you've seen the delicious meals that await you, let's talk about how you can make food preparation even easier with your air fryer. These tips will help streamline your cooking process, save time, and ensure you have delicious home-cooked meals within reach throughout the week. Whether you're a food prep pro or just starting out, these tips will help you get the most out of your air fryer and enjoy stress-free cooking all week long.

CONCLUSION

FINAL THOUGHTS ON DEEP FRYER COOKING AND ITS VERSATILITY

As we say goodbye to the culinary escapades chronicled in Fried to Perfection: The Ultimate Guide to Air Fryer Cooking, it's only fitting to pause and reflect on the remarkable journey we've taken together. In these pages, we've revealed the transformative power of deep fryer cooking – a culinary marvel that has forever changed the way we approach food preparation. From crispy treats that defy expectations to juicy masterpieces that excite the taste buds, the versatility of the air fryer is second to none. It's a tool that effortlessly balances comfort with creativity, health with enjoyment, and simplicity with sophistication. As we take our final bow, let's marvel at the sheer ingenuity of deep fryer cooking and celebrate the endless possibilities it offers for culinary discovery and expression.

ENCOURAGEMENT FOR READERS TO EXPLORE AND EXPERIMENT WITH THEIR FRYERS

But our journey does not end here; in fact, it's just getting started. As you close the cover of this cookbook and return to your own kitchen, I invite you to embrace the spirit of adventure and experimentation that has guided us thus far. Let your imagination run wild and don't be afraid to push the limits of what you thought was possible with your fryer. Whether you're diving into a new recipe, using your own recipe for an old favorite, or daring to come up with something completely unique, remember that the joy of cooking is in the journey itself. So put on your chef hat, roll up your sleeves and let your culinary creativity soar. The kitchen is your playground and the deep fryer is your faithful companion - so go ahead, explore, experiment and enjoy every delicious moment.

THANKING READERS FOR JOINING THE AIR FRYER COOKBOOK COOKING JOURNEY

Before we part ways, I want to express my deepest gratitude to you, dear reader, for embarking on this culinary odyssey with me. It was an honor and a privilege to be your guide as we journeyed through the delicious world of deep fryer cooking together. Your enthusiasm, curiosity and unwavering support have been the driving force behind every recipe, every tip and every word written on these pages. I am deeply grateful for the opportunity to share my passion for cooking with you and to witness the joy and satisfaction that deep fryer cooking has brought to your life. As you continue on your own culinary journey, may your kitchen be filled with laughter, love and the irresistible aroma of delicious food cooked to perfection. And remember, the recipes, techniques, and memories you've discovered on these pages will always be there to inspire and guide you. Here are many more delicious adventures shared around the table. Enjoy and happy cooking!

Printed in Great Britain
by Amazon